PROPERTY OF

The
TWELVE SIGNS OF THE ZODIAC
and Their Polarities

Zodiac, meaning "circle or cycle of animals," indicates the apparent path of the sun, moon, and planets through a defined swath of the various constellations. There are twelve astrological signs, each occupying 30 degrees of the 360-degree circle of the zodiac. An individual's zodiac sign (the part of the zodiac through which the sun was moving at the time of birth) is believed by some to be related to a person's defining characteristics.

This journal will identify each of the twelve "sun signs" and, importantly, each of their opposites. It is necessary to understand these contrasting signs in order to achieve balance in one's life.

For example, it can be useful for an Aries (independent, assertive) to learn from the complementary qualities of their Libra (diplomatic, interdependent) opposite on the zodiac circle. Understanding a Libra, or one's own "inner Libra," can therefore help an Aries on the path to balance and personal growth. The same can be said for every other sign and its corresponding opposite.

ARIES

March 21–April 19

· · · · · · · · · ✦ · · · · · · · · ·

Aries is the first sign of the horoscope wheel and the pioneer of the zodiac. Often leaders, Aries are trailblazing, competitive, and motivated. They are highly competent at multitasking and often have many different projects on their mind. Aries are forthright and can at times be a little too blunt. They can have a fiery temper, but when that energy is channeled properly, Aries can make the impossible happen. In love, Aries are passionate, impulsive, and all about initial attraction. Aries' energy and dynamism may be hard to keep up with, but if one is able to do so, they'll have a friend for life.

SYMBOL: The Ram
ELEMENT: Fire
RULING PLANET: Mars
COLOR: Red
GEM: Diamond
LOVE MATCHES: Sagittarius & Leo

Aries: Assertive, stubborn, courageous, impatient, ambitious

Balance with Libra: Diplomatic, relationship-oriented, sensitive to the needs of others

TAURUS

April 20–May 20

- - - - - - - - - ◆ - - - - - - - - -

Taurus is the second sign of the horoscope wheel and the anchor of the zodiac. The Taurus personality is smart, driven, and persistent. They can be the best friends, colleagues, and partners and are loyal and trustworthy. Taurus people value honesty above all else and are proud of their stable relationships. While they are hard workers, they also make sure to schedule in time for leisure and indulge in pleasure and sensuality. Being perfectionists, their attention to detail can make them overly critical. Taurus is ruled by Venus, the planet of love, so when it comes to intimacy, the Taurus personality is sensual, charming, and passionate.

SYMBOL: The Bull
ELEMENT: Earth
RULING PLANET: Venus
COLOR: Pink
GEM: Emerald
LOVE MATCHES: Cancer & Virgo

Taurus: Practical, overindulgent, dependable, stable, dedicated

Balance with Scorpio: Energetic, innovative, daring, intense

GEMINI

May 21–June 20

Gemini is the third sign of the horoscope wheel and the chameleon of the zodiac. The twins symbol illustrates how the Gemini personality can reveal different sides to the world and is adept at adjusting to different situations. Quick, witty, and dynamic, Gemini is a master of communication and excels at dialogue, public speaking, and socializing. While intelligent, Geminis also have a deep emotional side and love to love. Once they have chosen a partner, Geminis are loyal and dedicated and will keep a relationship fresh and exciting.

SYMBOL: The Twins
ELEMENT: Air
RULING PLANET: Mercury
COLOR: Yellow
GEM: Pearl
LOVE MATCHES: Aries & Leo

Gemini: Curious, affectionate, communicative, adaptable, scattered

Balance with Sagittarius: Philosophical, exploratory, spiritual

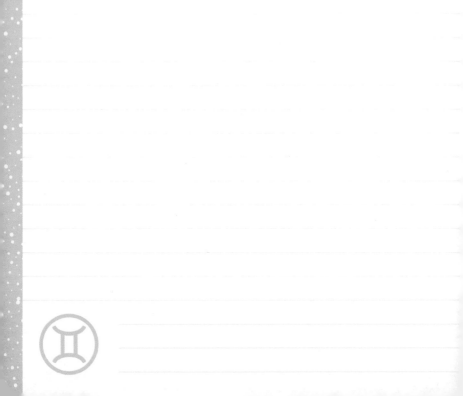

CANCER

June 21–July 22

Cancer is the fourth sign of the horoscope wheel and the natural nurturer of the zodiac. Like the crab, Cancer personalities tend to have a hard outer shell but are soft and vulnerable inside. A lot goes on internally, and being emotionally intelligent, Cancers can often intuit motivations, opinions, and emotions. Due to their overly sensitive nature, Cancers can be overwhelmed in large social gatherings and they much prefer to spend quality time with loved ones at home. Cancers are often introverted and have a rich imagination; therefore, while they like company, they also need time to be alone. Romantically, Cancers are warm, loving, and extremely loyal—at times, too much so.

SYMBOL: The Crab
ELEMENT: Water
RULING PLANET: Moon
COLOR: Violet
GEM: Ruby
LOVE MATCHES: Capricorn & Pisces

Cancer: Intuitive, nurturing, moody, home-loving, creative

Balance with Capricorn: Public-facing, career-oriented, serious, focused

LEO

July 23–August 22

········◆········

Leo is the fifth sign of the horoscope wheel and the natural leader of the zodiac. Bold and proud, the Leo personality is intense, energetic, and skilled at interpersonal interactions. Leos are kind and generous, have great self-esteem, and will lead from the heart. At times, they can come across as arrogant and aggressive, but when Leo energy is used properly, they can lead in such a way as to empower and inspire. When it comes to love, Leo likes to go all the way and is a true romantic.

SYMBOL: The Lion
ELEMENT: Fire
RULING PLANET: Sun
COLOR: Gold
GEM: Peridot
LOVE MATCHES: Libra & Aquarius

Leo: Courageous, bold, arrogant, proud, self-made

Balance with Aquarius: Humanitarian, innovative, progressive, political

VIRGO

August 23–September 22

· · · · · · · ◆ · · · · · · ·

Virgo is the sixth sign of the horoscope wheel and the masterful helper of the zodiac. Smart and sophisticated, Virgos are great at planning, big-picture thinking, and general practicalities. Virgo personalities like control, are good at organization, and tend to be perfectionists. Virgo's high standards can cause them to achieve great things but may also negatively affect their close relationships and lead them to be anxious and overwhelmed. Virgos are inspired by beauty. Being one of the more passionate signs of the zodiac, they appreciate having a physical connection with their partner.

SYMBOL: The Virgin
ELEMENT: Earth
RULING PLANET: Mercury
COLOR: Silver
GEM: Sapphire
LOVE MATCH: Cancer

Virgo: Organized, kind, loyal, critical, hardworking

Balance with Pisces: Spontaneous, playful, spiritual, accepting

LIBRA

September 23–October 22

· · · · · · · ◆ · · · · · · ·

Libra is the seventh sign of the horoscope wheel and the sign that brings balance to the zodiac. Symbolized by the scales, Libras bring harmony and fairness to all matters. The Libra personality is kind, lovable, and charming. They bring harmony to any situation and epitomize diplomacy. They have a tendency to want to please everyone, which leads them to overlook their own objectives. Being ruled by Venus, the planet of love, Libras are all about peace, love, and beauty, and they will search this out in all expressions of life.

SYMBOL: The Scales
ELEMENT: Air
RULING PLANET: Venus
COLOR: Blue
GEM: Opal
LOVE MATCH: Gemini

Libra: Diplomatic, artistic, indecisive, social, charming

Balance with Aries: Assertive, independent, pioneering, decisive

SCORPIO

October 23–November 21

• • • • • • • ◆ • • • • • • •

Scorpio is the eighth sign of the horoscope wheel and the most intense sign of the zodiac. While mysterious and secretive by nature, Scorpio personalities are full of energy, charm, and resourcefulness. Scorpios are passionate, powerful, charismatic, and transformational but also may be possessive or manipulative. Individuals born under this rich and powerful sign are great leaders, and there will never be a dull moment in their company. In love, the Scorpio may be cautious initially, but once in a relationship, the connection will be strong and passionate.

SYMBOL: The Scorpion
ELEMENT: Water
RULING PLANET: Mars
COLOR: Red
GEM: Topaz
LOVE MATCH: Sagittarius

Scorpio: Passionate, possessive, magnetic, obsessive, independent

Balance with Taurus: Stable, grounded, loyal, trustworthy

SAGITTARIUS

November 22–December 21

· · · · · · · · ◆ · · · · · · · ·

Sagittarius is the ninth sign of the horoscope wheel and the adventurer of the zodiac. Broad-minded and inquisitive, the Sagittarius is a straight shooter and will be on a quest through travel, inquiry, and constant change. Extroverted, enthusiastic, and optimistic, the Sagittarius has a great sense of humor and a good ability to connect with people. They have a tendency to overcommit and can therefore end up being reckless and taking risks that are too big. Sagittarius individuals are flirtatious and like to be single but may well end up being deeply loyal partners.

SYMBOL: The Archer
ELEMENT: Fire
RULING PLANET: Jupiter
COLOR: Purple
GEM: Turquoise
LOVE MATCHES: Aries & Leo

Sagittarius: Inspiring, confident, inquisitive, argumentative, encouraging

Balance with Gemini: Smooth communicator, witty, adaptable

CAPRICORN

December 22–January 19

· · · · · · · · ◆ · · · · · · ·

Capricorn is the tenth sign of the horoscope wheel and the master planner of the zodiac. Capricorns are determined and focused and are able to set and achieve their goals. Due to their ambitious nature, Capricorns may end up in prestigious public positions. They are family-oriented, hardworking, forward-thinking, and devoted but also can have a tendency to be unforgiving, materialistic, and calculating. Capricorns are responsible and appreciate traditional family values. Being the most serious-minded of the signs, they can be highly committed partners.

SYMBOL: The Goat
ELEMENT: Earth
RULING PLANET: Saturn
COLOR: Brown
GEM: Garnet
LOVE MATCHES: Taurus & Virgo

Capricorn: Practical, collected, hardworking, unforgiving, responsible

Balance with Cancer: Nurturing, sensitive, home-loving

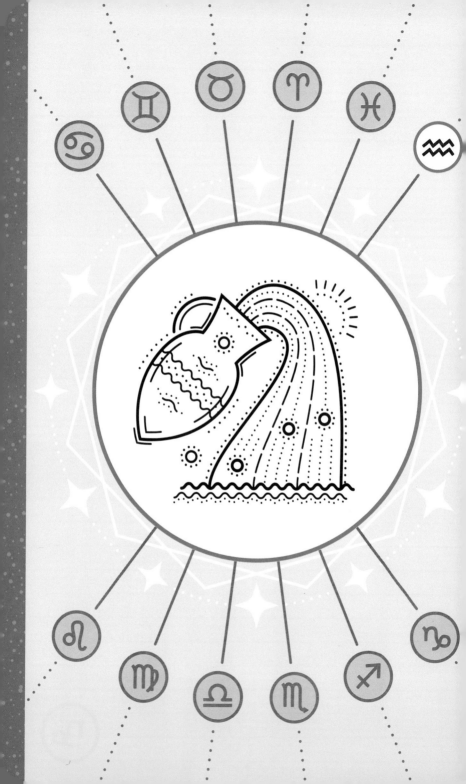

AQUARIUS

January 20–February 18

* * * * * * * ◆ * * * * * *

Aquarius is the eleventh sign of the horoscope wheel and the humanitarian of the zodiac. The progressive Aquarius personality is innovative and forward-thinking. Aquarius people are often engaged in philanthropy or are committed to a political cause. They are intelligent but can be closed or hesitant to express their emotions and may come across as a little strange at times. In love, Aquarius will choose friendships over romance and freedom over too much intimacy, as their commitment to the world tends to be more important to them.

SYMBOL: The Water Bearer
ELEMENT: Air
RULING PLANET: Uranus
COLOR: Turquoise
GEM: Amethyst
LOVE MATCHES: Aries & Libra

Aquarius: Progressive, innovative, emotionally guarded, supportive of causes

Balance with Leo: Expressive, strong leaders, assertive, traditional

PISCES

February 19–March 20

· · · · · · · ◆ · · · · · · ·

Pisces is the last sign of the horoscope wheel and the dreamer and healer of the zodiac. The Pisces personality is compassionate, imaginative, and artistic with a fervent interest in exploring the deeper meaning in life. Pisces are romantic, helpful, wise, and never superficial. They can accommodate the company of a wide variety of different personalities and are accepting of others. Due to their rich imagination and spiritual inclination, Pisces can lose touch with reality or may become self-pitying. Pisces are loving and giving when it comes to their romantic relationships. They need to feel an intimate and deep connection with their partners, and when they do, they are committed for life.

SYMBOL: The Fish
ELEMENT: Water
RULING PLANETS: Neptune & Jupiter
COLOR: Sea green
GEM: Aquamarine
LOVE MATCHES: Cancer & Scorpio

Pisces: Imaginative, wise, idealistic, gentle, compassionate

Balance with Virgo: Practical, precise, focused

INSIGHTS

A Mandala Journal

MANDALA
PUBLISHING

www.mandalaearth.com